THE
Washington
Redskins

Previous Books by Leonard Shapiro

Big Man on Campus:
John Thompson and the Georgetown Hoyas

Tough Stuff: The Man in the Middle (with Sam Huff)

Athletes for Sale (with Ken Denlinger)

THE
Washington
Redskins

Leonard Shapiro

ST. MARTIN'S PRESS
NEW YORK

Production Editor: Suzanne Magida
Production Manager: Kathy Fink

This book is in no way authorized, sponsored, or endorsed by the Washington Redskins or by the National Football League.

Library of Congress Cataloging-in-Publication Data

Shapiro, Leonard
    The Washington Redskins/Leonard Shapiro.
      p.   cm.
    ISBN 0-312-08519-2
    1. Washington Redskins (Football team)—Miscellanea.   I. Title.
GV956.W3S43   1992
796.332'64'09753—dc20   92-18469
                                            CIP

First Edition: September 1992
10 9 8 7 6 5 4 3 2 1

Books are available in quantity for promotional or premium use. Write to Director of Special Sales, St. Martin's Press, 175 Fifth Avenue, New York, N.Y. 10010, for information on discounts and terms, or call toll-free (800) 221-7945. In New York, call (212) 674-5151 (ext. 645).

To brave Vicky, for everything,
and to Jennifer, Emily, and Taylor for so much joy.

CONTENTS

ACKNOWLEDGMENTS

Many thanks to all my friends at the *Washington Post*, particularly Assistant Managing Editor, George Solomon, and Richard Justice, the best beat man in the NFL. Also thanks to the Washington Redskins public relations staff, Charlie Dayton, Mike McCall, John Autry, and Phyllis Hayes, my agent and dear friend Esther Newberg, and my multitalented editor at St. Martin's, George Witte.

INTRODUCTION

The love affair between the Washington Redskins and their faithful fans began almost immediately back in 1937, the team's initial season in the nation's capital.

Sammy Baugh can still vividly remember 10,000 Washingtonians boarding trains to New York and marching down Seventh Avenue upon their arrival, singing "Hail to The Redskins" as a prelude to the team's victory over the New York Giants at The Polo Grounds for the Eastern Division title. "Those people came out and supported us right away," Baugh said. "They just loved our football team."

George Preston Marshall, the team's original owner, made a football game in Washington a special event. He was the first in the NFL to field his own band, to have his own team fight song, and to offer tickets on a full-season basis. His halftime shows were extravaganzas; every Christmas Santa Claus showed up, occasionally hitching a ride on an elephant, and once parachuting into the stadium from a plane.

Marshall was a marketing genius who sold his franchise as "the team of the south," setting up a regional radio and television network that beamed the Redskins into southern Virginia, Georgia, South Carolina, and North Carolina where they still are the team of choice to this day.

Even in the lean years the team drew well, and in 1966 the Redskins began an unbroken streak of sellout games at RFK Stadium. Every regular season game since that season has been sold out. There are now over 44,000 names on a waiting list for season tickets.

True to the George Preston Marshall tradition, Redskins games are still a major social event. Up in the owner's box, it's not uncommon to see any number of the city's power elite. Down in the stands, hog noses and burgundy jerseys form the nucleus of the NFL's most distinctive dress code.

Quarterback Sammy Baugh (left) with first Redskins' owner George Preston Marshall (Associated Press).

Said CBS announcer John Madden, "It's the only show in town."

Now, fifty-five years after first arriving in Washington, the Redskins are nothing less than an institution, one of the NFL's most successful franchises, and of course, the defending world champions.

So why not a book of trivia for the people team owner Jack Kent Cooke describes "as the best bloody fans in all of football."

And so I give you 300 questions—a few no-brainers, a couple of "gimmes," and some that may send you to the history books—to test your knowledge and jar your memory of Redskins past and present.

—Leonard Shapiro
September 1992

WARM-UP

1   Who was the Redskin receiver Howard Cosell described as "that little monkey" in a Monday Night football game in 1987?

●

2   What defensive end was known as "The Dancing Bear"?

●

3   What linebacker was the subject of a 1960 CBS documentary narrated by Walter Cronkite?

●

4   What quarterback also had a brief acting career in Hollywood as the star of the series *King of the Texas Rangers*?

●

5   Who is the only Redskin coach ever to have an NFL stadium named in his honor?

●

6   Name the six members of the 1937 world champion Redskins in the Pro Football Hall of Fame.

●

7   True or false: Sonny Jurgensen holds the team record for highest percentage of passes completed in a season.

●

8   Who is the only offensive lineman in team history to score a touchdown?

●

9   What defensive back also serves as a spokesman for the South Carolina Wildlife Commission?

●

10   What safety went on to become athletic director at his own alma mater?

●

11   Name the player who had the longest career as a member of the Redskin organization.

●

12   Who scored the first touchdown in Redskin history?

●

13   What defensive lineman once hosted his own gourmet-cooking television show?

●

14 What assistant coach earned Pro Bowl honors in five of his eight NFL sesasons?

●

15 What offensive lineman has a twin brother who once played for the Los Angeles Raiders?

●

16 What Canadian Football League team did Joe Theismann play for?

●

17 What quarterback was an amateur magician and has been head coach of two NFL teams?

●

18 Name the five former Redskin coaches in the Hall of Fame.

●

19 Who is the leading career scorer in team history?
  a) Sammy Baugh
  b) John Riggins
  c) Mark Moseley
  d) Charley Taylor

●

20 Name the three Redskins who have played in three different decades.

●

21 Match the player with his alma mater:

Brig Owens	Prairie View
Ken Houston	Michigan
Pat Fischer	Cincinnati
Mike Bass	Nebraska

●

22 What was the major business of George Preston Marshall, the team's founder and first owner?

●

23 "Hail To The Redskins," written in 1937, is the oldest fight song in the NFL. Who wrote the words and music?

●

24 The No. 1 draft choice the Redskins traded to the Cleveland Browns for Bobby Mitchell in 1962 was used to select another famous player of that era. Name him.

25 What offensive lineman once played college basketball at Columbia?

26 Name the wide receiver who played sparingly in the George Allen era, but had an uncanny knack for blocking punts and placements.

27 What Redskin executive once was voted to the all-time Buffalo Bills defensive unit, was a four-time All-AFL safety, and used to mix motor oil with shampoo because he heard it would stop hair loss?

28 Name two of the most valuable members of the Redskin staff who owe their marital bliss to the team.

29 Name the Redskin assistant coaches who once were college teammates of head coach Joe Gibbs.

30 Who was the last Redskin named as The Pro Bowl's most valuable player?

31 Who holds the team record for interceptions in a season?

32 Who was the last Redskin to lead the NFL in rushing?

33 What rushing leader has the highest per-carry average in the team's history?
   a) John Riggins
   b) Bill Dudley
   c) Larry Brown
   d) Dick Todd

34 Who has the highest quarterback rating in team history?

35 This one-time, eighteenth-round draft pick in 1965 was a nine-time Pro Bowl selection. Name him.

36 George Allen held an open tryout for all-comers at Georgetown University in 1972, but only one player he signed that day ever made the team. Name him.

•

37 Who was the flakey Oklahoma running back who once roomed with Sam Huff, until they engaged in a fist fight in practice one day?

•

38 Name the receivers who once finished 1, 2, and 4 in the NFL, the highest ever for receivers on the same team.

•

39 Who was the first pure kicker ever selected in the first round of the NFL draft?

•

40 The 1981 draft yielded these six eventual starters for the Redskins in the 1980s. Name them.

•

41 Name the former free agent who went on to start as middle linebacker and also had a job as a deputy sheriff in the off-season.

•

42 The Redskins discovered this tight end while scouting his college teammate, Neil Lomax, at Portland State. Who was he?

•

43 Who was the Redskins' first opponent in their first game at RFK Stadium, then known as D. C. Stadium?

•

44 Who did the Redskins trade to the Philadelphia Eagles to obtain Hall of Fame quarterback Sonny Jurgensen?

•

45 Name the two rookies who made the roster in 1977, George Allen's final season in Washington.

•

46 Who was former Cowboy receiver Drew Pearson's teammate at South River High School in New Jersey?

•

47 What tight end was the creator of the Fun Bunch end-zone celebrations in 1982?

48 The Redskins acquired this Baltimore Colt running back in a draft-day trade for a second-round choice in 1981.

49 Who holds the team record for consecutive games played?

50 This defensive lineman was playing the tuba in his high school band when the football coach convinced him to try out for the team his senior year.

ARMED AND
DANGEROUS

Almost from the day Sammy Baugh stepped off the plane at National Airport in cowboy boots and a ten-gallon hat in 1937, the Redskins have had a tradition of greatness at the most important position of all—quarterback.

Baugh was known as "Slingin' Sam," a college hero at Texas Christian who played offense and defense for the Redskins, and also handled the punting from 1937 to 1952, when he retired to his Texas ranch. The Redskins won two NFL titles under Baugh and got to the championship game three more times. He led the league in passing six times and still holds the NFL record for punting average—51.4 yards. Baugh was inducted into the Hall of Fame in 1963.

In 1964, the Redskins traded Norman Snead to the Philadelphia Eagles for Sonny Jurgensen, and their offense would never be the same again. Playing on teams with mostly mediocre defense, Jurgensen turned RFK Stadium into a flying circus, with 400-yard passing games standard operating procedure. His targets over the years included Hall of Fame receivers Bobby Mitchell and Charley Taylor. Together, the three struck fear in the hearts of NFL defenders. Jurgensen was inducted into the Hall of Fame in 1983.

His best friend on the football team in the 1970s also was his main rival for the starting quarterback job, fiery Billy Kilmer, the first man George Allen acquired in trade when he arrived in 1971. Kilmer had none of Jurgensen's style or panache and threw a football that was just as likely to go end over end as it was to spiral. Yet, he ran the offense just the way Allen wanted—short passes and Larry Brown left, Larry Brown right—all the way to the team's first Super Bowl appearance in 1972.

9

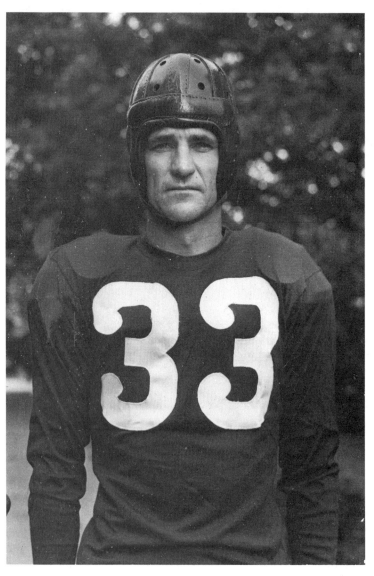

"Slingin' Sammy" Baugh (Associated Press).

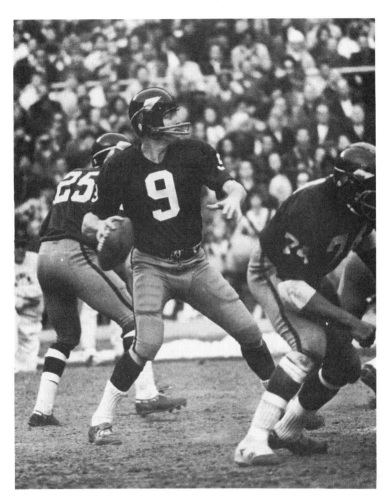

Sonny Jurgensen drops back to pass.

Early in the Sonny/Billy era, the Redskins had also acquired former Notre Dame star Joe Theismann, who was so eager to play his first few years in Washington that he volunteered to return punts. Theismann had to wait until the late '70s to get his turn behind center, and was the perfect mobile quarterback for the system installed by Joe Gibbs in 1981. Theismann led the team to two straight Super Bowls—and might still be playing if not for a freak accident in a Monday Night game against the New York Giants in 1985. He was tackled by Lawrence Taylor and broke a leg, which ended his career.

In 1987, Doug Williams literally came out of nowhere to lead the Redskins to another Super Bowl championship. A free agent signed for quarterback insurance, Williams replaced petulant Jay Schroeder that year and became a national hero, the first black quarterback to start—and then win—a Super Bowl against the Denver Broncos. Williams came back from a twisted knee early in the game to lead the Redskins to a 35-point, second-quarter barrage and was named the game's most valuable player.

In 1991, it was Mark Rypien's turn at the helm, and he clearly made the most of his opportunity. A question mark at the start of the '91 season, he silenced all the doubters week after memorable week with his deft passing and splendid on-field leadership, taking the Redskins to their third Super Bowl championship against the Buffalo Bills, winning the game MVP award to cap off a stunning season.

Jurgensen and Billy Kilmer, friends and rivals at quarterback.

Joe Theismann (Gary Cameron, *The Washington Post*).

Doug Williams, Super Bowl hero (Joel Richardson, *The Washington Post*).

Mark Rypien, today's star (John McDonnell, *The Washington Post*).

WARM-UP ANSWERS

1 Alvin Garrett.

2 Ron McDole.

3 Sam Huff.

4 Sammy Baugh.

5 Earl "Curly" Lambeau.

6 Owner, George Preston Marshall; coach, Ray Flaherty, quarterback, Sammy Baugh; running back, Cliff Battles; tackle, Turk Edwards; and end Wayne Millner.

7 False. Sammy Baugh set the record of 70.3 percent in 1945. Jurgensen is second at 64.1 percent in 1974.

8 Joe Jacoby.

9 Brad Edwards.

10 Mark Murphy, at Colgate.

11 Nate Fine, the team photographer from 1937 until his death in 1988.

12 Riley Smith, on a 60-yard interception return against the New York Giants on September 16, 1937. Smith also kicked two field goals and an extra point in the 13–3 Washington victory at Griffith Stadium.

13 Eric Williams.

14 LaVern "Torgy" Torgeson.

15 Raleigh McKenzie.

16 Toronto Argonauts.

17 Sam Wyche.

18 Ray Flaherty, Turk Edwards, Earl "Curly" Lambeau, Otto Graham, and Vince Lombardi.

19 a) Mark Moseley, with 1,207 points.

20 Sammy Baugh, Monte Coleman, and Don Warren.

21 Brig Owens, Cincinnati; Ken Houston, Prairie View; Pat Fischer, Nebraska; and Mike Bass, Michigan.

22 Marshall owned Washington D.C.'s Palace Laundry.

23 Words by Corrine Griffith Marshall, the owner's wife; music by Barnee Briskin, a Washington bandleader.

24 Ernie Davis.

25 George Starke.

26 Bill Malinchak.

27 George Saimes, the team's director of college scouting.

28 General manager, Charley Casserly and special teams coach, Wayne Sevier both married team employees.

29 Quarterback coach, Rod Dowhower; tight end coach, Rennie Simmons, and special teams coach, Wayne Sevier.

30 Joe Theismann, in 1983.

31 Dan Sandifer, with 13 in 1948.

32 Larry Brown in 1970.

33 d) Dick Todd, with a 6.5 yard average in 1946.

34 Sammy Baugh, 109.7 in 1945.

35 Chris Hanburger.

36 Herb Mul-Key.

37 Joe Don Looney.

38 Charley Taylor, Bobby Mitchell, and Jerry Smith, in 1967.

39 Charlie Gogolak of Princeton, in 1966.

40 Mark May (first round); Russ Grimm (3); Dexter Manley (5); Charlie Brown (8); Darryl Grant (9); and Clint Didier (12).

41 Neal Olkewicz.

42 Clint Didier.

43 The New York Giants, who rallied from a 21–0 deficit to win 42–21, on October 1, 1961.

44 Norm Snead.

45 Safety, Mark Murphy and running back, Clarence Harmon.

46 Joe Theismann.

47 Rick "Doc" Walker.

48 Joe Washington.

49 Center, Len Hauss, 196 straight games.

50 Fred Stokes.

FIRST AND TEN

1 This one-time tie-maker from Cyprus became famous in Super Bowl VII for trying to throw a pass that almost cost the Miami Dolphins a victory. Who was he, and what Redskin defensive back recovered the ball?

•

2 Name the kicker who graduated from the U.S. Coast Guard Academy.

•

3 In four years at Penn State, he played strong safety, tailback, fullback, defensive end, cornerback, and linebacker, and later started as linebacker for the Redskins. Name him.

•

4 The Redskins' latest Super Bowl trophy is on display at what well-known Washington restaurant?

•

5 What starting outside linebacker is now working in the team's scouting department?

•

6 He was a nine-letter man at the University of Wisconsin and a tight end who was one of Sonny Jurgensen's favorite targets. Who was he?

•

7 Name the former No. 1 draft choice who Vince Lombardi once cut for arriving late for a team meeting in training camp.

•

8 Name the six Los Angeles Rams acquired in a single trade by George Allen in 1971.

•

9 Who was known to his teammates as "The Tasmanian Devil" before the Redskins traded him to the Dallas Cowboys in 1988?

•

10 What draft choices did the Redskins have to give up to the then St. Louis Cardinals in order to sign free-agent defensive tackle Dave Butz in 1975?

•

11 Which of the following NFL coaches did not play for the Redskins?

a) Sam Wyche (Tampa Bay)
b) Bruce Coslet (New York Jets)
c) Jack Pardee (Houston)
d) Don Shula (Miami)

●

12 What is the team record for longest pass completion without a touchdown?

●

13 Who holds the Super Bowl record for most yards with a returned fumble?

●

14 In the storied Redskin–Cowboy rivalry, only one game has ever gone into overtime. What Redskin scored the winning touchdown?

●

15 Who did the Redskins play and what was the final score in the highest-scoring Monday Night game ever?

●

16 Who did the Redskins defeat to record Joe Gibbs' first victory as a head coach in 1981?

●

17 How much did a box seat on the 50-yard line cost at a Redskin game in 1937, the team's first year in Washington?

●

18 Who was the last Redskin defensive back to reach double figures in interceptions?

●

19 What player made the most Pro Bowl appearances as a Redskin?

●

20 What defensive lineman scored a fourth-quarter touchdown in the 1982 NFC championship game?

●

21 Who holds the team record for the longest kickoff return?

●

22 This well-known broadcaster was former general manager Bobby Beathard's college roommate. Name him.

●

23 Who were the first father-son ever to play in the NFL?
•

24 Who were the first two Redskin running backs to each exceed 100 yards rushing in the same game?
•

25 Hall of Famer Turk Edwards shared the same number with what fiery Redskin quarterback of the 1970s?
•

26 What Redskin was also a former Super Bowl MVP playing for a different team?
•

27 What famous running back was known as "Bullet"?
•

28 What current assistant coach played safety for the 1963 world champion Chicago Bears?
•

29 The Redskins have played only one scoreless tie in team history. Name the opponent and the year.
•

30 "The Little General" was the shortest Redskin quarterback to lead the NFL in passing. Who was he?
•

31 Who was the third player selected in the 1975 baseball draft, which he played professionally for four years before signing with the Redskins?
•

32 The Redskins have trained in this sleepy Pennsylvania college town since 1963. Name the town and the college.
•

33 What defensive lineman was the nephew of a former Republican secretary of agriculture?
•

34 What current assistant coach was Don Coryell's first starting quarterback at San Diego State?
•

35 Name the five Redskin running backs who gained over 1,000 yards in a season.
•

36 What Redskin quarterback won a Heisman Trophy?
a) Sonny Jurgensen
b) Gary Beban
c) Billy Kilmer
d) Joe Theismann

●

37 Several 1991 Redskins played at rather obscure colleges. Match the player with his school.

Monte Coleman	Emporia State
Ricky Sanders	Central Arkansas
John Brandes	Southwest Texas State
Kelly Goodburn	Cameron

●

38 Name the only four rookies to start on opening day for a Joe Gibbs Redskin team.

●

39 What Redskin player, almost a scratch golfer, won the NBC Celebrity Golf Classic in Lake Tahoe, Nevada, in 1990?

●

40 Name the two Outland Trophy winners who started the 1991 season with the Redskins.

●

41 Linebacker Matt Millen has played on four Super Bowl championship teams. Name the teams and the years.

●

42 When Auburn's Bo Jackson won the Heisman Trophy in 1985, this tight end was chosen his team's most valuable player.

●

43 Match the Redskin with his favorite offseason sport.

Chip Lohmiller	Hiking
Gerald Riggs	Tae kwon do
Raleigh McKenzie	Tennis
Markus Koch	Golf

●

44 This receiver and D.C. native was a starting point guard on the Notre Dame basketball team.

●

45 Though he hasn't played baseball since high school, who was the quarterback taken by the Cleveland Indians in the 1989 draft?

•

46 What player is an avid hunter and fisherman and once owned his own sporting-goods retail store?

•

47 In his first NFL game against the Steelers in 1986, he made a tackle on kickoff coverage despite losing his helmet running down the field. Name him.

•

48 In 1990, he was the only player in the NFL to rush, receive, and throw for a touchdown. Who is he?

•

49 Who is the current assistant coach who recorded the last interception in American Football League history?

•

50 Name the two players who combined for the longest pass play in NFL history.

THE BRAIN TRUST

Jack Kent Cooke The owner of the Washington Redskins has been involved with the football team ever since he bought a 25 percent share in the franchise from George Preston Marshall in 1960. He became majority owner in 1974, and in 1979 moved from California to Virginia to begin to run the organization himself. In 1981, Cooke hired Joe Gibbs, an obscure assistant coach from the San Diego Chargers, as his head coach, which began the organization's most successful era in its history. Cooke, a communications and real estate magnate, has never been hesitant to go the extra mile and to spend the extra dollar to improve the team; Gibbs describes him as the best owner in the National Football League.

Joe Gibbs The Redskins' head coach is a driven man, a workaholic who still occasionally sleeps on the office couch during the season. Though he began his head coaching career with a five-game losing streak, his record since has moved him into the elite ranks of NFL coaches, with four Super Bowl appearances and three championships. He's also the winningest coach in Redskins history and one of the most innovative offensive minds in the league. He uses a one-back offense, likes to call his tight end an H-back, and is known for his creative game plans and masterful adjustments in the heat of battle.

Charley Casserly The team's general manager originally came to the Redskins as an unpaid intern to George Allen. He hoped to learn enough to move on as an assistant coach, but Casserly soon developed an eagle eye for talent that blossomed under former GM Bobby Beathard. Casserly was the man who originally spotted All-Pro tackle Joe Jacoby, convincing the team to sign him as a free agent. When Beathard

Jack Kent Cooke, the Redskins' owner.

Joe Gibbs on the sideline (John McDonnell, *The Washington Post*).

Charley Casserly, general manager (John McDonnell, *The Washington Post*).

left for San Diego in 1989, Casserly got the job, and the Redskins haven't missed a beat since. He was instrumental in building the 1991 Super Bowl championship team, and a bold move on draft day last April allowed the Redskins to move up in the first round and select Heisman Trophy winner Desmond Howard with their No. 1 pick.

JOHN RIGGINS:
DIESEL POWER

The setting seemed so appropriate. The day John Riggins got the telephone call telling him he had just been selected to the Pro Football Hall of Fame, he was in Cancun, Mexico, helping to promote Jose Cuervo Rum at an event being billed by the company as the world's biggest beach party.

It seemed that every day had been a party for John Riggins ever since he arrived in the National Football League, a peach-fuzz rookie from the University of Kansas who was the No. 1 draft choice of the New York Jets in 1971. Early on, perhaps the year he wore his hair in a Mohawk-style cut, it became quite clear this gregarious small-town kid with big-time ability and a whimsical nature was no ordinary running back.

"If this was gonna' be a Jack Armstrong contest, I wasn't gonna' get in," Riggins said when told about the Hall of Fame vote in January, 1992. "I was Igor or Dr. Frankenstein all in one, doing my own experiments."

Riggins joined the Redskins as a free agent in 1976 and was used primarily as a blocking back his first two seasons under George Allen. As he got older, he got better, and just a tad wilder.

He once told Supreme Court Justice Sandra Day O'Connor to "loosen up, Sandy baby" before he passed out under a table at a banquet. He took a full year off in a contract dispute (1980), once told reporters he worked on his balance by learning to walk on a tightrope in his backyard, and came out for a bow at midfield after a 186-yard rushing performance against the Minnesota Vikings in the 1982 playoffs.

He was a big man, 6 feet 2 inches, almost 250 pounds, with a massive upper body and powerful legs known to Redskin fans as "The Diesel." There were three 1,000-yard seasons

"Riggo," John Riggins, going for yardage (Dudley M. Brooks, *The Washington Post*).

Riggins breaks away from the Dolphins' Don McNeal for his 43-yard touchdown run in Super Bowl XVIII (*United Press International*).

after he was 30, an age when most NFL backs are limping toward their orthopedic surgeons. He played fourteen years, retiring with a gentle push from Joe Gibbs after the 1985 season as the NFL's sixth leading rusher (11,352 yards) and third-leading touchdown scorer (116).

His most memorable accomplishments occurred in the strike-shortened 1982 season. Going into the playoffs, he told Gibbs to "load up the wagon" and give him the ball. He then had four straight 100-yard plus playoff games, including a 38-carry, 166-yard, record-breaking performance in Washington's 27–17 Super Bowl XVII victory over the Miami Dolphins. His 43-yard, fourth-quarter touchdown run put the Redskins ahead for good, and he was named the game's MVP.

When he was told he'd been elected to the Hall of Fame, Riggins' response at first seemed a bit lighthearted, just like the man. "I'm kind of a carefree, effervescent kind of person," he said that day. "I never take anything too seriously. But there's something about this, when the window opens and they let you in. It touches your soul."

Just as John Riggins did on so many carries, for so many years.

JOHN RIGGINS, CAREER STATISTICS

Year	Team	Rushing					Receiving				
		No	Yds	Avg	Lg	TD	No	Yds	Avg	Lg	TD
1971	NY Jets	180	769	4.3	25	1	36	231	6.4	32	2
1972	NY Jets	207	944	4.6	40	7	21	230	11.1	67t	1
1973	NY Jets	134	482	3.6	15	4	23	158	6.9	19	0
1974	NY Jets	169	680	4.0	34	5	19	180	9.5	32	2
1975	NY Jets	238	1,005	4.2	42	8	30	363	12.1	34	1
1976	Washington	162	572	3.5	15	3	21	172	8.2	18	1
1977	Washington	68	203	3.0	12	0	7	95	13.6	53	2
1978	Washington	248	1,014	4.1	31	5	31	299	9.6	33	0
1979	Washington	260	1,153	4.4	66t	9	28	163	5.8	23	3
1981	Washington	195	714	3.7	24	13	6	59	9.8	22	0
1982	Washington	177	553	3.1	19	3	10	50	5.0	11	0
1983	Washington	375	1,347	3.6	44	24*	5	29	5.8	14	0
1984	Washington	327	1,239	3.8	24	14	7	43	6.1	11	0
1985	Washington	176	677	3.8	51	8	8	18	3.0	8	0
NFL Totals		2916	11,352	3.9	66t	104	250	2,090	8.1	67t	12
Redskin Totals		1988	7,442	3.8	66t	79	121	928	7.4	53	6
Jet Totals		928	3,880	4.2	42	25	129	1,162	9.0	67t	6

*NFL Record

PLAYOFF STATISTICS

Year	Rushing					Receiving				
	No	Yds	Avg	Lg	TD	No	Yds	Avg	Lg	TD
1976	7	30	4.3	16	0	4	29	7.2	13	0
1982	136	610	4.5	43t	4	1	15	15.0	15	0
1983	87	306	3.5	23	6	1	1	1.0	1	0
1984	21	50	2.4	8	2	0	0	0.0	0	0
Totals	251	996	4.0	43t	12	6	45	7.5	15	0

ALL-TIME RUSHERS

		Years	Attempts	Yds	TDs
1	Walter Payton	13	3,838	16,726	110
2	Tony Dorsett	12	2,936	12,739	77
3	Eric Dickerson	9	2,783	12,439	88
4	Jim Brown	9	2,359	12,312	106
5	Franco Harris	13	2,949	12,120	91
6	**John Riggins**	**14**	**2,916**	**11,352**	**104**

FIRST AND TEN
ANSWERS

1 Garo Yepremian tried to throw the pass. Mike Bass recovered for the Redskins.

2 Curt Knight.

3 Rich Milot.

4 Duke Zeibert's restaurant.

5 Mel Kaufman.

6 Pat Richter.

7 Ray McDonald.

8 Defensive tackle, Diron Talbert; running back, Jeff Jordan; guard, John Wilbur; linebacker, Myron Pottios; linebacker, Jack Pardee; linebacker, Maxie Baughan.

9 Dean Hamel.

10 Two No. 1 choices and a No. 2 choice.

11 b) Bruce Coslet.

12 Joe Theismann threw 84 yards to Alvin Garrett in 1983.

13 Mike Bass, 49 yards against the Miami Dolphins in Super Bowl VII.

14 Billy Kilmer on November 2, 1975.

15 Green Bay beat the Redskins, 48–47.

16 Chicago, 24–7.

17 $7.50.

18 Paul Krause in 1964.

19 Chris Hanburger, nine appearances.

20 Darryl Grant.

21 Larry Jones, 102 yards against the Eagles on November 24, 1974.

22 John Madden.

23 Frank "Tiger" Walton played offensive line for the Redskins in the 1940s, his son Joe joined the team as a tight end in 1957.

24 George Rogers (104 yards) and John Riggins (103) against the Cardinals in 1985.

25 No. 17, the same as Billy Kilmer.

26 Jake Scott, MVP of Super Bowl VII for the Miami Dolphins.

27 Bill Dudley.

28 Defensive coordinator Richie Petitbon.

29 New York Giants, October 1, 1939.

30 Eddie LeBaron in 1958.

31 Jay Schroeder.

32 Carlisle, Pennsylvania; Dickinson College.

33 Dave Butz, nephew of Earl Butz.

34 Special teams coach Wayne Sevier.

35 Larry Brown, John Riggins, George Rogers, Mike Thomas, and Earnest Byner.

36 b) Gary Beban, in 1967.

37 Monte Coleman, Central Arkansas; Ricky Sanders, SW Texas State; John Brandes, Cameron; Kelly Goodburn, Emporia State.

38 Darrell Green, Mark May, Andre Collins, Ed Simmons.

39 Mark Rypien.

40 Tracy Rocker and Mo Elowonibi.

41 Raiders in 1980 and '83; 49ers in 1989, Redskins in 1991.

42 Ron Middleton.

43 Chip Lohmiller, golf; Gerald Riggs, tennis; Raleigh McKenzie, tae kwon do; Markus Koch, golf.

44 Joe Johnson.

45 Cary Conklin.

46 Monte Coleman.

47 Ravin Caldwell.

48 Earnest Byner.

49 Emmitt Thomas, who had three interceptions in Super Bowl IV before the AFL and NFL merged.

50 Frank Filchock passed 99 yards to Andy Farkas in 1939 against the Steelers.

SECOND AND FIVE

1 Who holds the Redskin record for most sacks in one game? Against what team?

●

2 What Redskin running back holds the NFL record for carries in a game?

●

3 Name the Redskins only two No. 1 picks from the University of Maryland.

●

4 Redskin receivers have led the NFL in pass receptions four times. Name the players and the years.

●

5 Who is the first native Alaskan to play in the NFL?

●

6 The Redskins made a draft-day trade with what team to move to the fourth pick in the first round, enabling them to take Heisman Trophy winner Desmond Howard of Michigan in 1992?

●

7 What brainy defensive lineman from the 1970s majored in mathematics at the University of Colorado?

●

8 The Redskins have sold out every home game since:
   a) 1963
   b) 1966
   c) 1972
   d) 1978

●

9 Name Mike Patrick's sidekick on ESPN's Sunday night pro football coverage.

●

10 Name Dexter Manley's coach at Oklahoma State.

●

11 The 1991 Redskins are one of only three teams to finish an NFL season at 17–2. Name the other two.

●

12 The Redskins have only selected two players in the first round of the NFL draft once, in 1961. Name the players they picked.

13 Joe Gibbs is one of five coaches to make at least four appearances in the Super Bowl. Name the other four.

•

14 The Redskins opened the 1991 season with eleven straight victories. Name the last NFL team to accomplish that feat, and the year.

•

15 The Redskins allowed only nine sacks in 1991. Name the only three teams who ever did a better job protecting the quarterback.

•

16 Name the only man who had a higher quarterback rating than Mark Rypien in 1991.

•

17 Name the Redskin running-back tandems that each gained 600 yards or more rushing in a single season.

•

18 Only two other Redskin receivers have more yardage than Gary Clark's 7,830. Name them.

•

19 What *Washington Post* columnist was the first media man to jump on the team's bandwagon in 1991?

•

20 Name the running back acquired by George Allen in 1973 who once called former Dallas coach Tom Landry a "plastic man."

•

21 Who were George Preston Marshall's three original partners in the Boston Braves franchise in 1932?

•

22 This eighth-round draft choice in the NFL's initial college draft in 1936 went on to become a Hall of Famer.

•

23 The Redskins very nearly finished winless in 1961. Name the quarterback who engineered the team's only victory in the last game of the season and the team they beat.

•

24 What running back and special team ace broke his neck in his last NFL game in 1977 and now runs a successful seafood restaurant in his native Louisiana?

•

25 What former world-record holder in the 100-yard dash spent the 1963 season as a Redskin wide receiver?

•

26 A total of forty-four Redskins joined the armed forces in World War II, but only one man was killed in action. Name him.

•

27 What former Redskin coach also founded Washington's famous Touchdown Club?

•

28 Name the seven members of the 1982 Fun Bunch.

•

29 What former assistant coach was known as "Boss Hog"?

•

30 Name the running back who was the first black player at the University of Alabama.

•

31 Name the running backs who had brothers who also played in the NFL.

•

32 What offensive lineman obtained in 1983 was picked ahead of Walter Payton in the 1975 draft?

•

33 What is former Redskin quarterback Babe Laufenberg's real name?

•

34 What offensive tackle and original Hog ever allowed a sack in his final two seasons at the University of Pittsburgh?

•

35 Where was John Riggins when he learned he'd been selected to the Pro Football Hall of Fame?

•

36 True or false: Of the forty-nine Redskins who played in Super Bowl XVII, twenty-six joined the team as free agents.

•

37 Before Art Monk accomplished the feat in 1985, who was the last man to have back-to-back 1,000-yard receiving seasons?

●

38 Name the two Redskins who scored all the points in the team's 26–3 NFC title game victory over the Dallas Cowboys in 1972.

●

39 Who was the first player George Allen traded for when he came to Washington in 1971?

●

40 Name the seven Redskins selected for the 1986 Pro Bowl.

●

41 Defensive lineman Dick Modzelewski played for the Redskins for two seasons before moving on to the New York Giants. What was his nickname?

●

42 This Hall of Famer and former Redskin coach was an All-American in football and basketball in the same season.

●

43 Acquired in a trade with the New England Patriots, this linebacker returned three fumbles for touchdowns in his Redskin career. Name him.

●

44 Vic Janowicz, a promising running back from Ohio State, was forced to retire from football in 1956 after two seasons in Washington. Why?

●

45 Sammy Baugh once described him as "the best end I ever threw to." Who was he?

●

46 This rookie went 83 yards with a kickoff in a preseason game against the Rams the first time he handled the football in the NFL.

●

47 Name the Redskin defensive back who earned stardom with the New York Jets in Super Bowl III.

●

48 Pick the quarterback who ran for over 1,800 yards in his NFL career.

a) Billy Kilmer
b) Sammy Baugh
c) Joe Theismann
d) Frank Filchok

●

49 Chuck Drazenovich went both ways in his first five years in the league. What positions did he play?

●

50 This current NFL head coach was George Allen's offensive coordinator.

HOG HEAVEN

It began as a joke and wound up as an institution. Little did offensive line coach Joe Bugel know that when he began calling his offensive linemen "Hogs" back in the 1982 season, a tradition of excellence was about to begin.

"A Hog," Bugel once said, "is a guy who gets down and does a dirty job without wanting to be beautiful."

The Hogs began making a name for themselves in the drive to the 1982 Super Bowl, clearing a path for fullback John Riggins to grind out yard after yard off tackle left, off tackle right, holding their ground to protect quarterback Joe Theismann as he dropped back to the pass.

By 1992, only Joe Jacoby, Jeff Bostic, and Don Warren were still playing, but the Hogs are still very much alive and snorting.

The original Hogs featured twelve players, including Riggins "because he has the personality of a Hog," offensive tackle George Starke once said.

"My greatest honor," Riggins said that season, fully mindful of the power of pork.

The original Hogs and their colleges:

> Center: Jeff Bostic, Clemson
> Guard: Fred Dean, Texas Southern
> Guard: Russ Grimm, Pittsburgh
> Guard: Mark May, Pittsburgh
> Guard: Ron Saul, Michigan State
> Tackle: Joe Jacoby, Louisville
> Tackle: George Starke, Columbia
> Tackle: Gary Puetz, Valparaiso
> Tackle: Don Laster, Tennessee State
> Tight end: Don Warren, San Diego State
> Tight end: Rick Walker, UCLA
> Fullback: John Riggins, Kansas

Offensive line coach Joe Bugel, with some of his Hogs (John McDonnell, *The Washington Post*).

Joe Jacoby, one of the original Hogs (Bill Snead, *The Washington Post*).

SECOND AND FIVE
ANSWERS

1 Diron Talbert, four against the Giants in 1975; Dexter Manley, four against the Giants in 1988.

2 Jamie Morris, 45 against the Bengals in 1989.

3 Quarterback, Jack Scarbath in 1953; running back, Ed Vereb in 1956.

4 Bobby Mitchell, 71 in 1962; Charley Taylor, 72 in 1966 and 70 in 1967; Art Monk, 106 in 1984.

5 Mark Schlereth.

6 Cincinnati Bengals.

7 Bill Brundige.

8 b) 1966.

9 Joe Theismann.

10 Jimmy Johnson.

11 1978 Steelers, 1986 Giants.

12 Tackle, Joe Rutgens of Illinois; quarterback, Norm Snead of Wake Forest.

13 Don Shula, 6; Tom Landry, 6; Chuck Noll, 4; and Bud Grant, 4.

14 1985 Bears.

15 1988 Dolphins, seven sacks; 1970 49ers and 1975 Cardinals, eight sacks.

16 49er Steve Young, 101.8 to Rypien's 97.9.

17 Earnest Byner (1,048) and Ricky Ervins (680) in 1991; George Rogers (1,093) and John Riggins (677) in 1985; John Riggins (1,347) and Joe Washington (772) in 1983; Joe Washington (916) and John Riggins (714) in 1981; and Larry Brown (948) and Charley Harraway (635) in 1971.

18 Charley Taylor (9,140) and Art Monk (10,984).

19 Tony Kornheiser.

20 Duane Thomas.

21 Larry Doyle, a New York stockbroker, Jay O'Brien, a New York investment banker, and Vincent Bendix, an auto-supply man from South Bend, Indiana.

22 Wayne Millner.

23 Norm Snead helped the Redskins beat Dallas, 34–24.

24 Bob Brunet.

25 Frank Budd.

26 Running back Keith Birlem, killed in battle in 1943.

27 Arthur J. "Dutch" Bergman.

28 Rick Walker, Charlie Brown, Otis Wonsley, Clarence Harmon, Don Warren, Alvin Garrett, and Virgil Seay.

29 Joe Bugel.

30 Wilbur Jackson.

31 Benny Malone (brother Art) and Keith Griffin (brothers Archie and Ray).

32 Ken Huff.

33 Brandon Hugh.

34 Mark May.

35 Cancun, Mexico.

36 True.

37 Bobby Mitchell in 1963–64.

38 Charley Taylor and Curt Knight.

39 Billy Kilmer.

40 Gary Clark, Darrell Green, Russ Grimm, Joe Jacoby, Dexter Manley, Jay Schroeder, and Art Monk.

41 Little Mo.

42 Otto Graham at Northwestern.

43 Brad Dusek.

44 He suffered a head injury in a car wreck during training camp in 1956.

45 Hugh "Bones" Taylor.

46 Dick James.

47 John Sample.

48 c) Joe Theismann.

49 Middle linebacker and fullback.

50 Ted Marchibroda of the Indianapolis Colts.

INTERMISSION

ART MONK: MR. REDSKIN

With five games left in the 1990 regular season, the Washington Redskins were drifting through their schedule at 6–5, seemingly destined for a third straight season out of the National Football League playoffs. That's when Art Monk took matters into his own hands—and mouth.

A man who relished his privacy, preferred avoiding the media, and felt more fearful of public speeches than lowering his shoulder into a 240-pound linebacker in front of 55,000 crazed RFK Stadium football fans finally decided to speak up.

On a Saturday night before a critical game against the Miami Dolphins, the Redskins had just finished their traditional snack of cheeseburgers, fries, and soft drinks when Monk got out of his chair in a hotel meeting room and asked the coaches to leave. He had something important to say. Joe Gibbs and his staff asked no questions, walked out the door, and never looked back.

That night, Monk reminded his teammates of their mediocre record and told them they were flirting with another season out of the playoffs. He told them they were better than that and said he thought there were enough good players in the room to accomplish their ultimate goal. Yet, for some reason, he said, shaking his head, they were losing too many close games.

A man of few words on his best day, Monk summed it up quickly. A player who had the well-earned reputation as the most fanatical worker of any Redskin in the history of the franchise told his teammates he was personally rededicating himself to football, and strongly suggested that they all would be wise to do the same. It was time, he told them, to stop all the talking and to start performing. Then he sat down.

Art Monk, in action and in person.

"That room was very quiet," tight end Ron Middleton recalled. "It made an impression, and not just because it was anything too profound he said. It was just that it came from Arthur. He's the type who usually leads by example. But if he stands up and says he's rededicating himself—as if he needs to—what can the rest of us do?"

The next day, Art Monk led by example. He caught ten passes against the Dolphins, two for touchdowns, and the Redskins routed Miami, 42–10. They won four of their last five games, made the playoffs, and surprised a favored Philadelphia Eagle team on the road in the first round of the playoffs before being eliminated by the 49ers.

After that short speech, the Redskins decided to include a players-only meeting on the night before every game, home or away. Monk didn't stand up again, preferring to let other older veterans like Monte Coleman or Jeff Bostic do the talking. But anyone who heard Monk that night before the Miami game will also tell you that the effects of that speech not only saved the 1990 season, but also carried over into the next year, one that ended with the Redskins winning their third Super Bowl since the quiet wide receiver joined the team as a first-round draft choice in 1980, a converted running back from Syracuse University.

Ask anyone about Monk and they'll tell you the same stories about his almost maniacal approach to the game, the great pride he takes in catching passes, and leveling potential tacklers with devastating effectiveness. In the off-season, Monk works out five days a week. He lifts weights in the morning, runs sprints in the afternoon, then jogs three miles wearing a weight belt at night. During the season, he'll often be found running on a treadmill before practice, then jogging in the evening when he gets home. His weight hasn't fluctuated more than five pounds since his hurdling days at White Plains (N.Y.) High School. He still does the same time in the 40-yard dash—4.5 seconds—he had as a rookie. And always, he's the man the Redskins look to when a game is on the line, just the way he prefers it.

"I like having pressure on me," he once told an interviewer. "I like for the team to be relying on me. That makes me want to perform. I pride myself on people being able to count on me."

Many of those people also will tell you he has virtually no ego in their locker room, that he says not much more to his team-mates than he does to the legion of frustrated reporters who have been turned down for interview requests over the years.

"He's got nothing to hide," said his friend and agent, Brig Owens, a Redskin defensive back in the 1970s. "He's just un-comfortable talking about himself. I don't think he thinks he's as good as everyone thinks he is. And he also knows it can end at any moment, and so he concentrates on what he thinks is important to him—getting ready to play."

Said Monk before the Super Bowl, "I don't consider myself a standout player. When I see myself, it doesn't look very spe-cial to me."

Over the years, Monk has turned down scads of big-money offers to give a speech here, schmooze with the corporate types there. Owens recalled sitting next to him at a banquet honoring another Redskin great, Assistant General Manager Bobby Mitchell. Monk had agreed to say a few words to a large gathering, but as the time drew closer for him to stand and talk, Owens said he felt Monk's knees shaking under the table.

"He said, 'feel my hands, Brig.' I did. They were definitely sweating. But he got up there and calmly gave his speech. No problem once he had to go. Getting there was the hard part."

In 1992, Monk should become the all-time leading receiver in NFL history, and if he stays healthy, could put numbers on the board that may never again be equaled. He's got 801 catches, second only to Steve Largent's 819. He's also caught a pass in 132 straight games, third on that all-time list, and this season also should become the fifth player in history to surpass 11,000 receiving yards for a career. The Hall of Fame? Probably in his first year of eligibility five years after he retires.

Monk is a second cousin to legendary jazz great Thelonious Monk and was a competent musician himself in high school, playing bass guitar, tuba, trombone, and drums before football moved him in another direction. He's a fussbudget who's worn the same pair of game shoes for most of the last seven years, who wears the same receiver gloves he used when he broke into the league, who goes to sleep by 11 P.M. almost every night, who thinks a sweet for dessert is a major splurge, who religiously consults with massage therapists and chiropractors every week during the season, who literally climbs mountains—well, steep hills anyway—to prepare himself for the rigors of an NFL season.

He's also heavily involved in the Washington, D.C. community. He works with the homeless, and his summer football camps also provide college scholarship money for kids in the area. Yet, as usual, he doesn't talk about this or many other of his other numerous charitable endeavors, including Special Olympics.

"He's the only guy on this team who can walk into a room and get absolute respect from everyone in that room," said wide receiver Gary Clark. "He *is* the Washington Redskins."

ART MONK: CAREER STATISTICS

Year	No	Yds	Receiving Avg	Receiving Lg	Receiving TD
1980	58	797	13.7	54t	3
1981	56	894	16.0	79t	6
1982	35	447	12.8	43	1
1983	47	746	15.9	43t	5
1984	*106	1,372	12.9	72	7
1985	91	1,226	13.5	53	2
1986	73	1,068	14.6	69	4
1987	38	483	12.7	62	6
1988	72	946	13.1	46t	5
1989	86	1,186	18.8	60t	8
1990	68	770	11.3	44	5
1991	71	1,049	14.8	64t	8
Totals	801	10,984	13.7	79t	60

*NFL Record

ART MONK: PLAYOFF STATISTICS

Year	No	Yds	Avg	Lg	TD
1983	8	121	15.1	40t	2
1984	10	122	12.2	35	0
1986	18	241	13.4	48	2
1987	1	40	40.0	40	2
1990	12	207	17.3	40	2
1991	15	252	16.8	31	1
Totals	64	983	15.2	40t	7

ART MONK: SINGLE-GAME HIGHS

Catches

13 (168) vs Detroit	11/04/90	10 (92) vs Miami	12/02/90
13 (230) vs Cincinnati	12/15/85	10 (200) vs San Francisco	09/10/84
11 (136) vs St. Louis	12/16/84	10 (122) vs Chicago	12/30/84
11 (104) vs Buffalo	11/25/84		

THIRD AND TWO

1   John Riggins broke this fellow Hall of Famer's career rushing records at the University of Kansas.

●

2   Sonny Jurgensen was unable to play in Super Bowl VII because of what injury?
a) Sprained ankle
b) Dislocated shoulder
c) Torn Achilles tendon
d) Bruised ribs

●

3   What Hall of Fame linebacker came out of retirement to work as the team's player coach under Vince Lombardi in 1969?

●

4   What was Sammy Baugh's salary and signing bonus in his rookie season?

●

5   Who was the first Redskin ever named the NFL's rookie of the year?

●

6   Return man Joe Scudero shared the same nickname as a famous New York Yankee shortstop.

●

7   What quarterback spent three years with the Redskins without ever throwing a regular-season pass?

●

8   George Allen once hired Ed Boynton, a former Long Beach, California policeman as his chief of security. What was his nickname?

●

9   At the time, George Allen was the only NFL coach to have what perk written into his contract?

●

10   Larry Brown attended what junior college for two years?

●

11   What Redskin was given an exemption to play in the 1992 Kemper Open golf tournament?

●

12   Name the position kicker Mark Moseley played in college at Stephen Austin.
    a) Halfback
    b) Cornerback
    c) Quarterback
    d) Middle linebacker

●

13   What tight end was known as "Frog" and caught 41 passes in 1985?

●

14   What running back has a son who played on an NCAA championship basketball team in 1991 and 1992?

●

15   This linebacker originally made his reputation with the Baltimore Colts and was known as "Mad Dog." Name him.

●

16   Who was the Redskins' starting middle linebacker in the 1972 Super Bowl?

●

17   What team did Jack Pardee leave in 1978 to coach the Redskins?

●

18   What was the price of a Redskin season ticket in their first season in Washington in 1937?
    a) $7.50
    b) $12
    c) $36
    d) $42

●

19   What team did George Allen leave to become head coach of the Redskins in 1971?

●

20   Name the former Colt head coach who also coached Charley Taylor and Jerry Smith in college.

●

21   What coach has the poorest won-lost record with the Redskins?

●

22   What jersey number did Hall of Fame running back Cliff Battles wear?

23   Joe Theismann came to the Redskins from this team for what price?

24   Joe Gibbs started his head coaching career in 1981 with a memorable streak. What was it?

25   Who holds the team record for passes thrown in a single game?

26   What tight end was once a starting quarterback at the University of Maryland?

27   They called this 1970s wide receiver from West Virginia University "Lightning." Who was he?

28   George Allen once described this center as "the best long snapper in football." Name him.

29   Name the only Amherst graduate ever to play for the Redskins.

30   This long, tall defensive end and special team standout from the 1970s shares his name with the Redskins' most hated rival. Name him.

31   What defensive lineman has starred in commercials for Diet Coke and McDonalds?

32   Who was the team's head coach when Pat Fischer joined the Redskins?

33   This great New York Giant running back failed a tryout as a defensive back with the Redskins in 1953.

34   Larry Brown gained 888 yards rushing as a rookie but finished second to what running back for rookie of the year honors in 1969?

35 What starting offensive tackle in Super Bowl VII was signed originally as a free agent?

●

36 General manager Charley Casserly came to the organization as an intern under what coach?

●

37 Bobby Mitchell played college football at the University of Illinois. What team drafted him, and in what round?

●

38 What Redskin coach shares the same name as a former U. S. president?

●

39 What was Speedy Duncan's real name?

●

40 What was Ken Houston's first job after retiring from football?

●

41 What former Kansas City All-Pro offensive lineman came to Washington at the end of his career in 1974?

●

42 It was only natural that this long-time Redskin trainer attended Lamar University in Beaumont, Texas. Who is he?

●

43 Since 1937, the Redskins have used seven No. 1 draft choices to pick a quarterback. Name them.

●

44 What freakish play occurred in the Redskins' 15–14 loss to the Los Angeles Rams in the 1945 NFL championship game?

●

45 When was the Redskins Alumni Association organized?

●

46 One season after he was named the NFL's coach of the year, this head coach was fired. Who was he?

●

47 Against what team did Charley Taylor become the all-time reception leader in NFL history?

●

48 Name the two teams that defeated the Redskins in the 1991 season.

49   Who was the sports editor of the *Washington Post* when the Redskins came to town in 1937?

50   What linebacker was a fierce special teamer in the 1970s and began his pro career in Canada?

GEORGE ALLEN: THE FUTURE IS NOW

When George Herbert Allen arrived to take over as head coach of the Redskins in 1971, he told victory-starved Washingtonians the future was now, then showed them exactly what he was talking about.

A man who believed rookies had no place on a football field, he immediately began trading draft choices for veteran players, the better to win now and worry later. The winning began that very first season when Allen's "Over The Hill Gang" advanced to the playoffs. In 1972, the team made its first appearance in the Super Bowl, losing to the Miami Dolphins, 14–7.

Allen was an eccentric character with a penchant for secrecy and skullduggery. Spies were everywhere, particularly when his team was about to face the hated Dallas Cowboys. Reporters were frequently barred from his closed practices, the better to prepare his team without all those pesky distractions.

Allen also was one of the game's great innovators. He was the first head coach to have a full-time special teams coach, and one of the first to employ situation substitution on defense. He was a pioneer in the use of extra defensive backs and linebackers—depending on down and distance.

His players were fiercely loyal to the man some in the press called "Nixon with a whistle." He paid them well and often prolonged many of their careers at a time when no other teams were interested in their skills. Team President Edward Bennett Williams once said of Allen's spending habits, "I gave him an unlimited expense account, and he exceeded it."

Eventually, Allen's trade-now personnel policies left the Redskins' cupboard mostly bare, and he stunned the football

George Allen, with President Richard Nixon (Associated Press).

world when he refused to sign a new contract and left to coach the Los Angeles Rams in 1978.

Allen was fired in Los Angeles even before the start of his first regular season there, and never coached in the National Football League again. He did surface in the old U.S. Football League, and in 1990, well into his 70s, he coached the Long Beach State college team. On New Year's Eve, 1990, he collapsed and died at his home in Palos Verdes, California, a football coach to the very end.

THIRD AND TWO
ANSWERS

1 Gale Sayers.
2 c) Torn Achilles tendon.
3 Sam Huff in 1969.
4 $8,000 salary and a $500 signing bonus.
5 Charley Taylor in 1964.
6 Scooter.
7 Sam Wyche.
8 "Double 0," as in 007.
9 A chauffeur-driven limousine.
10 Dodge City.
11 Mark Rypien.
12 c) Quarterback.
13 Clint Didier.
14 Calvin Hill, whose son Grant starred for Duke's national champs in 1991 and 1992.
15 Mike Curtis.
16 Myron Pottios.
17 Chicago Bears.
18 a) $7.50
19 Los Angeles Rams.
20 Frank Kush.
21 Herman Ball, 4-16.
22 No. 20.
23 Miami Dolphins for a 1976 No. 1 choice.
24 The team started 0–5.
25 Jay Schroeder, 58 against the Giants in 1985.
26 Mike Tice.
27 Danny Buggs.
28 Ted Fritsch.
29 Jean Fugett.

30 Dallas Hickman.

31 Charles Mann.

32 Otto Graham.

33 Alex Webster.

34 Calvin Hill.

35 Terry Hermeling.

36 George Allen.

37 Cleveland Browns, in the eighth round in 1958.

38 Mike Nixon (1959–60).

39 Leslie.

40 Teaching and coaching high school football.

41 Jim Tyrer.

42 Lamar "Bubba" Tyer.

43 Sammy Baugh, 1937; Larry Isbell, 1952; Jack Scarbath, 1953; Ralph Guglielmi, 1955; Don Allard, 1959; Richie Lucas, 1960; and Norman Snead, 1961.

44 Sammy Baugh's pass from the end zone hit the goal post for a safety under rules of that era.

45 October 15, 1958.

46 Jack Pardee, coach of the year in 1979, fired after the 1980 season.

47 Taylor caught the then-record 634th reception in the final game of the 1975 season against the Eagles.

48 Cowboys and Eagles.

49 Shirley Povich.

50 Pete Wysocki.

FOURTH AND ONE

1   Who had a 75-yard run on one play and an interception return of 76 yards for a touchdown on another to clinch the NFL East title in 1937?

•

2   What former LSU star only played two seasons for the Redskins but holds the single-season record for interception return yards?

•

3   True or false: Sonny Jurgensen holds the team record for career touchdown passes.

•

4   How many first-round picks did the Redskins have in the 1970s?

•

5   What offensive lineman was offered a football scholarship to Eastern Washington without the school's coaches ever having seen him play a single game in high school?

•

6   What reserve running back plays the drums, likes to juggle, and was the No. 3 rusher in Division I-AA history when he left Appalachian State in 1986?

•

7   The Chicago Bears fielded three Hall of Famers on the offensive line in their 1937 NFL championship game against the Redskins. Who were they?

•

8   Former Georgia Coach Vince Dooley once called this man "the finest defensive back I've ever coached."

•

9   When he first joined the Redskins as a free agent in April, 1991, he wanted to play running back. Name him.

•

10   What was the original name of the team fight song "Hail to The Redskins"?

•

11   Why did star running back Cliff Battles leave the Redskins before the start of the 1938 season?

•

12   Who were the first three Redskins named to play in the Pro Bowl in 1950?

13 What's the largest margin of a Redskin victory in the team's playoff history?

14 Who holds the record for longest run from scrimmage against the Redskin defense?

15 What player holds four team record returning kickoffs—most career yards, most yards in a season, highest average return, and most career returns?
   a) Brian Mitchell
   b) Mike Nelms
   c) Dick James
   d) Rickie Harris

16 What player led the NFL in touchdown scoring in 1938, with six?

17 The Redskins selected what long-time starter with their first choice in 1979 (in the fourth round)?

18 Who scored the team's first touchdown of a 35-point second quarter in Washington's victory over Denver in Super Bowl XXII?

19 What tight end came to the Redskins from the Houston Oilers the same year as his best friend and college teammate, Ken Houston?

20 What offensive lineman of the 1950s went by the nickname "Slug"?

21 These 1973 teammates were popular with area jewelers and geologists. Name them.

22 What center from the University of Georgia once served as president of the NFL Players Association?

23 What multitalented running back's son now plays the same position for the Cleveland Browns?

24 What brainy Redskin quarterback once served as athletic director at Yale?

25 Name the running back for George Allen who once was married to "Peter Pan."

26 What running back did the Redskins send to the Cleveland Browns in exchange for Earnest Byner?

27 Who did the Redskins beat on Pearl Harbor Day, December 7, 1941, and where was the game played?

28 Art Monk caught a pass in 132 straight games, the third longest streak in NFL history. Who's ahead of him?

29 Joe Gibbs beat what team in 1987 to become the winningest coach in Washington history?

30 Name the four leading sackers in team history.

31 What cornerback attended Cerritos Junior College in California, the same school Joe Gibbs played his first two years of college football?

32 What tenth-round draft choice in 1950 served in the Korean War and was wounded twice?

33 Who was runner-up to Jim Plunket for the Heisman Trophy in 1970?

34 What famous New York baseball announcer was the play-by-play man for the national radio broadcast of the Redskins 14–6 victory over the Chicago Bears in the 1942 NFL championship game?

35 What were two of the nicknames Billy Kilmer went by?

36 Who was the starting receiver on the 1955 Redskins who shares the same name as a popular television host?

•

37 What Hall of Fame quarterback destroyed the Redskins in the 1943 title game against the Bears?

•

38 Who holds the team record for most 100-yard games in a season?
- a) Larry Brown
- b) John Riggins
- c) George Rogers
- d) Earnest Byner

•

39 You can call him Joe Johnson, the name he legally changed to honor the family who raised him. What was his name when he played at Notre Dame?

•

40 What Redskin defensive lineman with a spring in his step originally went to Paducah (Kentucky) Community College on a basketball scholarship?

•

41 What valuable member of the team's equipment staff is a member of the Softball Hall of Fame as a catcher and has a delicious nickname?

•

42 Until defensive lineman Bobby Wilson was selected in the 1991 draft, who was the last Washington defender taken with a No. 1 draft choice?

•

43 What's the lowest round the Redskins have ever started the draft?

•

44 Vince Lombardi once had a unique cure for Larry Brown fumbling the football. What was it?

•

45 In his first game, he returned an interception 72 yards for a touchdown against the Rams. Name him.

•

46 What was the longest run of Joe Theismann's career?

47 What Redskin coach converted Charley Taylor from half-back to split end?

48 How long was John Riggins' famous fourth-quarter touch-down run against the Miami Dolphins in Super Bowl XVII?

49 Where did George Allen start his coaching career?

50 What famous college coach had Eddie LeBaron at the College of the Pacific?

WHEELING AND DEALING

The Redskins have been involved in some of the NFL's most stunning trades over the last 30 years. Here's a sample of their more memorable moves:

1962 Redskins trade their No. 1 choice in the draft (Syracuse running back Ernie Davis) to Cleveland for running back Bobby Mitchell, integrating the football team for the first time. Mitchell eventually switched to wide receiver and was named to the Hall of Fame in 1983.

1964 Redskins trade quarterback Norman Snead and defensive back Claude Crabb to the Philadelphia Eagles for quarterback Sonny Jurgensen, who turns the Redskins into a high-scoring offensive machine. Jurgensen was named to the Hall of Fame in 1983.

1964 Redskins trade popular running back Dick James to the New York Giants for middle linebacker Sam Huff, who anchors the defense for the next five years. Huff was named to the Hall of Fame in 1982.

1971 Redskins send first- and third-round choices in the 1971 draft, plus third- through seventh-round choices in '72 draft, plus linebacker Marlin McKeever to the Los Angeles Rams for defensive tackle Diron Talbert, guard John Wilbur, linebackers Mo Pottios, Jack Pardee, and Maxie Baughan, running back Jeff Jordan, and the Rams fifth-round choice in the '71 draft. The "Over the Hill Gang" is born.

1971 Redskins send linebacker Tom Roussel, a fourth- and eighth-round choice in the '71 draft to the New Orleans Saints for quarterback Billy Kilmer, who led the team to the Super Bowl in 1972.

1973 Redskins send five players, offensive lineman Jim Snowden, tight end Mack Alston, defensive end Mike Fanucci, receiver Clifton McNeil, and safety Jeff Severson to Houston Oilers for safety Ken Houston. Houston was named to the Hall of Fame in 1986.

1981 Redskins trade a No. 1 pick in 1982 draft for a No. 3 pick in 1981 (guard Russ Grimm), a No. 5 pick in 1981 (defensive end Dexter Manley), and a No. 2 pick in 1982 (cornerback Vernon Dean).

1988 Redskins trade quarterback Jay Schroeder to Los Angeles Raiders for offensive tackle Jim Lachey, now considered the best offensive lineman in the NFL.

1992 Redskins trade their two No. 1 draft choices (the sixth and twenty-eighth picks) to Cincinnati for Bengals first-round choice (fourth pick) and select wide receiver Desmond Howard, the Heisman Trophy winner from Michigan.

Author's Note The Redskins under Joe Gibbs and general managers Bobby Beathard and Charley Casserly also had great success bringing in free agents. Among the free agents on the 1991 Redskins were center Jeff Bostic (1980); wide receiver Gary Clark (1985); punter Kelly Goodburn (1991); tackle Joe Jacoby (1981); linebacker Wilbur Marshall (1988); and cornerback Alvoid Mayes (1990).

Plan B free agents on the Super Bowl champions included center Mark Adickes; tight end John Brandes; tackle Ray Brown; safety Danny Copeland; safety Brad Edwards; defensive tackle Jumpy Geathers; safety Terry Hoage; receiver Stephen Hobbs; cornerback Martin Mayhew; tight end Ron Middleton; linebacker Matt Millen; quarterback Jeff Rutledge; and defensive end Fred Stokes.

FOURTH AND ONE
ANSWERS

1 Cliff Battles.

2 Dan Sandifer, 258 yards in 1948.

3 False. Sammy Baugh had 187 touchdown passes, Jurgensen had 179.

4 None.

5 Ed Simmons.

6 John Settle.

7 Tackle Joe Stydahar, guard Danny Fortmann, and guard George Musso.

8 Safety Terry Hoage.

9 Safety Danny Copeland.

10 The Redskins March.

11 Team owner George Preston Marshall refused him a $1,000 raise, and Battles left to become an assistant coach at Columbia.

12 Bill Dudley, Harry Gilmer, and Paul Lipscomb.

13 44 points in a 51–7 victory over the Rams on January 1, 1984.

14 Bobby Mitchell, then with the Browns, 90 yards on November 15, 1959.

15 b) Mike Nelms.

16 Andy Farkas.

17 Don Warren.

18 Ricky Sanders.

19 Alvin Reed.

20 Casimir Witucki.

21 Ken Stone and Walter Rock.

22 Len Hauss.

23 Terry Metcalf, father of Eric Metcalf.

24 Frank Ryan.

25 Tommy Mason, whose former wife, Cathy Rigby, played "Peter Pan" on Broadway.

26 Mike Oliphant.

27 The Redskins beat the Eagles, 20–14, at Griffith Stadium.

28 Steve Largent with 177 games and Ozzie Newsome with 150.

29 Chicago Bears, 27–13, in a divisional playoff game. It was Gibbs' 70th victory.

30 Dexter Manley, 97.5; Charles Mann, 77; Dave Butz, 59.5; Diron Talbert, 56.

31 Sidney Johnson.

32 Eddie LeBaron.

33 Joe Theismann.

34 Russ Hodges.

35 Whiskey and Furnace Face.

36 Johnny Carson.

37 Chicago Bears' Sid Luckman.

38 a) Larry Brown.

39 Joe Howard.

40 Jumpy Geathers.

41 William "Lego" Lamb.

42 Darrell Green.

43 Eighth, in 1972, when they selected Moses Denson of Maryland-Eastern Shore.

44 He made him carry a football everywhere he went for one week during training camp.

45 Darrell Green.

46 37 yards for a touchdown against the Giants.

47 Otto Graham.

48 43 yards.

49 Morningside College in Iowa.

50 Amos Alonzo Stagg.

OT

1   What offensive lineman from Michigan State opened a popular downtown bar and restaurant when he retired?

●

2   What punt-blocking specialist came out of retirement in 1976 to rejoin the team?

●

3   What offensive tackle from Notre Dame went on to become the head coach at the University of Virginia?

●

4   A great schoolboy athlete at Washington's McKinley Tech, what running back played in Washington for the 1979 season?

●

5   What outside linebacker made his reputation with the Green Bay Packers before coming to the Redskins in 1973?

●

6   Pat Fischer and Ron McDole were long-time Redskin teammates and alumni of what midwestern university?

●

7   In what three categories did Bullet Bill Dudley lead the NFL in 1946?

●

8   How many times did Sammy Baugh lead the NFL in passing?

●

9   True or false: John Riggins was the team's leading scorer in the 1982 postseason.

●

10   He was an integral part of the Redskins from 1945 to 1953, playing both ways at center and linebacker. Who was he?

●

11   How big was Wee Willie Wilkin?

●

12   What receiver from the 1950s was drafted out of Loyola of Los Angeles on the eighteenth round?

●

13   What brilliant center from Northwestern played for the Bears and Rams before joining the Redskins in 1971?

●

14 What defensive back was shot to death in 1957 when he tried to break up a fight in a bar he owned in San Francisco?

●

15 Name the three rookie running backs who made up the team's starting backfield in 1957.

●

16 When did the Redskins begin to play in what is now called RFK Stadium? What was the final outcome of the first game?

●

17 Name the only player ever to lead the team in rushing and receiving in the same season.

●

18 Who was the rookie running back who led the team in rushing in 1975?

●

19 What is the longest run from scrimmage in team history?

●

20 True or false: Sonny Jurgensen is the team's all-time passing yardage leader.

●

21 Sam Huff played five seasons for the Redskins and now broadcasts their games on the radio. What's his real first name?

●

22 What first-term Virginia congressman is the son of a former Washington coach?

●

23 What former team president and part-owner hired Vince Lombardi to coach the team in 1969?

●

24 What original Hog retired after the 1991 season and became an assistant coach?

●

25 John Riggins joined the Hall of Fame in the summer of 1992. Name the other members of the class.

●

26 Who was the first Redskin lineman honored with his own day?

•

27 What Hall of Famer suffered a career-ending knee injury while running off the field following a coin toss?

•

28 Name the man Edward Bennett Williams succeeded as team president in 1965.

•

29 Three players had record-setting days in Super Bowl XXII against the Broncos. Who were they?

•

30 Name the coach who gave Joe Gibbs his first NFL coaching job.

•

31 Who was the team's starting placekicker in Super Bowl XXII?

•

32 Name the former Redskin assistant who coached Paul Hornung at Notre Dame and Larry Brown in his rookie season in Washington.

•

33 Who was the first former player to be named the team's head coach?

•

34 What nickname did the media give George Allen's Los Angeles Rams acquisitions in 1972?

•

35 Name the only Redskin to intercept a pass against the Dolphins in Super Bowl XVII.

•

36 Vince Lombardi immediately traded for this former Packer defensive back when he came to the Redskins in 1969.

•

37 Only seven of the team's seventeen head coaches had winning records. Name them.

•

38 Name the only member of the 1981 team selected for the Pro Bowl.

39 What linebacker has one of the most recognizable faces in Japan because of his appearances in a number of magazine ads there?

40 What long-time public relations director of the Redskins now is a publicist at the University of Maryland?

41 Who was known as "the peach from Long Beach"?

42 What assistant coach was head coach of the St. Louis Cardinals from 1980–85?

43 What Hall of Famer led the team in rushing in 1964 and 1965?

44 Who caught 73 passes in 1988, 12 for touchdowns?

45 Who led the team in interceptions in 1957?

46 What team knocked the Redskins out of the playoffs in George Allen's first season?

47 Who was the last Heisman Trophy winner before George Rogers to play for the Redskins?

48 What running back came to Washington from the New York Jets in 1972 and now is an accomplished painter?

49 Joe Gibbs was a national 35-and-over champion in this sport.

50 Who was the last man selected in the 1992 draft?

OT ANSWERS

1 Fran O'Brien.
2 Bill Malinchak.
3 Don Lawrence.
4 Lonnie Perrin.
5 Dave Robinson.
6 Nebraska.
7 Rushing, interceptions, and punt returns.
8 Six times, in 1937, 1940, 1943, 1945, 1947, 1949.
9 False. Alvin Garrett had five touchdowns, Riggins had four.
10 Al DeMao.
11 He was 6 feet 6 inches and weighed 280 pounds.
12 Gene Brito.
13 George Burman.
14 Roy Barni.
15 Don Bosseler, Jim Podoley, and Ed Sutton.
16 The Redskins lost the opening game of the 1961 season to the Giants, 24–21.
17 Joe Washington in 1981.
18 Mike Thomas.
19 Billy Wells ran 88 yards for a touchdown against the Cardinals in 1954.
20 False. Joe Theismann is first with 25,206 yards, Jurgensen is second with 22,585.
21 Robert.
22 George Allen Jr.
23 Edward Bennett Williams.
24 Russ Grimm.
25 Al Davis, John Mackey, and Lem Barney.
26 Al DeMao, November 2, 1952.
27 Turk Edwards.
28 Leo DeOrsey.

29 Quarterback, Doug Williams with 340 passing yards; receiver, Ricky Sanders with 193 receiving yards; and running back Tim Smith with 204 rushing yards.

30 Don Coryell, who hired Gibbs to coach the St. Louis Cardinal running backs in 1973.

31 Ali Haji-Sheikh.

32 George Dickson.

33 Turk Edwards.

34 Ramskins.

35 Mark Murphy.

36 Tom Brown.

37 Ray Flaherty, 47–16–3; Dutch Bergman, 6–3–1; Dudley DeGroot, 14–5–1; Dick Todd, 5–4; Vince Lombardi, 7–5–2; George Allen, 67–30–1; Joe Gibbs, 118–53.

38 Mike Nelms.

39 Kurt Gouveia.

40 Joe Blair.

41 Jerry Smith.

42 Jim Hanifan.

43 Charley Taylor.

44 Ricky Sanders.

45 Don Shula.

46 49ers.

47 Gary Beban.

48 George Nock.

49 Racquetball.

50 Matt Elliot.

THE LAST WORD

George Preston Marshall, addressing the fans in New York before the team's 49–14 victory over the New York Giants at the Polo Grounds for the NFC East title in 1937: "The Indians have come to reclaim Manhattan Island."

Sammy Baugh, when asked if the outcome might have been different if Redskin receiver Charley Malone had held on to a certain touchdown pass in the first quarter of the team's 73–0 loss to the Bears in the 1940 title game: "Hell yes, the score would have been 73–6."

Shirley Povich on the final outcome that day: "It reminds us of our first breathless visit to the Grand Canyon. All we could say is 'There she is and ain't she a beaut.' When they hung up that final score at Griffith Stadium yesterday, all we could utter was: 'There it is, and wasn't it awful.'"

Sonny Jurgensen, learning of his trade to the Redskins in 1963: "You've got to be kidding."

Otto Graham, after sending in kicker Charlie Gogolak to kick a field goal in the final seconds of a 72–41 victory over the Giants in 1966: "Gogolak needed the practice."

Vince Lombardi the day he was hired as the team's head coach in 1969: "I will demand a commitment to excellence and to victory. I came to Washington because it is the capital of the world and I plan to make it the football capital."

George Allen: "Losing is like death."

George Allen: "The future is now."

Team president Edward Bennett Williams on Allen: "I gave him an unlimited expense account, and he exceeded it."

Joe Gibbs after winning Super Bowl XVII: "I feel like all the people who accomplished what they want to do. I'm thrilled, elated, proud, and I feel good for all the people who've been pulling for the Redskins."

John Riggins after Super Bowl XVII: "Ron is the president, but I'm the king."

John Riggins to Supreme Court Justice Sandra Day O'Connor: "Loosen up, Sandy baby."

Doug Williams after the Redskins beat the Broncos, 42–10, in Super Bowl XXII: "Joe Gibbs and Bobby Beathard didn't bring me in to be the first black quarterback in the Super Bowl. They brought me in to be the quarterback of the Washington Redskins."

Jack Kent Cooke after the Redskins beat the Buffalo Bills, 37–24, in Super Bowl XXVI: "I have so much pride in Joe Gibbs and the coaching staff. And we have the best bloody fans on the face of the earth."